The Big Book of
Things That Go

DK | Penguin Random House

DK UK
Senior editor Gill Pitts
US Senior editor Shannon Beatty
Managing editor Laura Gilbert
Managing art editor Diane Peyton Jones
Producer, pre-production Nadine King
Producer Srijana Gurung
Art director Martin Wilson
Publisher Sarah Larter
Publishing director Sophie Mitchell
Consultant Phil Hunt

DK India
Editor Ishani Nandi
Assistant editor Anwesha Dutta
Art editor Shipra Jain, Yamini Panwar
Assistant art editor Jaileen Kaur
DTP designers Md Rizwan,
Vijay Kandwal, Bimlesh Tiwary
Managing editor Alka Thakur Hazarika
Senior managing art editor Romi Chakraborty
CTS manager Balwant Singh
Production manager Pankaj Sharma
Jacket designers Kartik Gera, Dheeraj Arora
Picture researcher Nishwan Rasool

Original project editor Caroline Bingham
Original art editor Sara Hill
Senior editor Sheila Hanly

First American Edition, 1994
This edition published in the United States in 2016 by
DK Publishing, 345 Hudson Street, New York, New York 10014

A catalog record for this book is available from the Library of Congress.
ISBN: 978-1-4654-4509-4

DK books are available at special discounts when purchased in bulk for sales
promotions, premiums, fund-raising, or educational use. For details, contact: DK
Publishing Special Markets, 345 Hudson Street, New York, New York 10014
SpecialSales@dk.com

Printed and bound in China

A WORLD OF IDEAS:
SEE ALL THERE IS TO KNOW
www.dk.com

Picture credits The publisher would like to thank the following for their kind permission to reproduce their photographs: (Key: a-above; b-below/bottom; c-centre; f-far; l-left; r-right; t-top). **1 Corbis**: Photolibrary. **4 123RF. com**: federicofoto (cl); Dmitriy Sladkov (cla). **Dorling Kindersley**: John Wilkes, Model Exhibition, Telford (tl). **5 Corbis**: Photolibrary (cra). **Dreamstime.com**: Shaiful Rizal Mohd Jaafar (bl). **6 Dreamstime.com**: Zkruger (t). **7 Dreamstime.com**: Djidji (cr); Rui Matos (t). **8 123RF.com**: Robert Wilson (cl). **Dreamstime.com**: Konstantinos Moraitis (t). **First Waste**, Hendon, London (br). **9 Robert Harding Picture Library**: Adam Woolfitt (crb). **10 Dreamstime.com**: Ukrid Yenpetch (cr). **Robert Harding Picture Library**: Ian Griffiths (br). **The Image Bank**: (cl). **Zefa** (bl). **11 123RF.com**: cyoginan (crb); Steve Estvanik (tl). **Zefa** (tr). **12 Corbis**: Adam Jahiel (cla). **Dreamstime.com**: Johnhill118 (t). **The Image Bank** (cl). **Zefa** (cr). **13 Alamy Images**: John Elk III (b). **Dreamstime.com**: Benjamin Rowland (clb). **14 123RF.com**: Robert Keenan (cl). **Dreamstime.com**: Marilyn Barbone (b). **15 123RF.com**: Kasto (b). **Tony Stone Images**: Alastair Black (t). **16 Dorling Kindersley**: Igor Dolgov (b). **17 Corbis**: Photolibrary (cr). **Balloon Base** (Bristol - UK) (br). **The J. Allan Cash Photolibrary** (clb); (bl). **19 Zefa**: Orion Press (bl). **20 Caterpillar** (cr); (cl). **Terex Equipment Ltd** (tr). **21 123RF.com**: Baloncici (cl). **22 Dreamstime.com**: Vladimir Bryzgin (b). **23 123RF.com**: Dmitriy Sladkov (bl). **Dreamstime.com**: Rui Matos / Rolmat (cl). **Tadano-Faun** (b). **David MacKrill Engineering Ltd** (cr). **24 123RF.com**: Scott Betts (cl); Stepan Popov (cra). **The J. Allan Cash Photolibrary** (cr). **Quadrant** (b). **25 Dreamstime.com**: Cobia (tl); Photodynamx (cl). **Quadrant** (t). **26 123RF.com**: federicofoto (cl). **27 Alamy Images**: IAN MARLOW (tr). **The Aviation Picture Library**: Austin J. Brown (cl). **Oshkosh Truck Corporation** (b). **28 123RF.com**: Gunter Nezhoda (cr). **Dreamstime.com**: Shaiful Rizal Mohd Jaafar (t). **Pete Biro** (t). **29 123RF.com**: gors4730 (tr). **Corbis**: Duomo (b). **30 Dorling Kindersley**: John Wilkes, Model Exhibition, Telford (cra). **Rex Shutterstock**: Geoffrey Robinson (c). **Terex Equipment Ltd** (tl). **31 Corbis**: Kieran Doherty / Reuters (t). **NASA** (clb). **Dorling Kindersley would also like to thank**: Action Vehicles at Shepperton Studios, Middlesex; AirBourne Aviation at Popham Airfield, Nr Basingstoke; Benford Ltd, Warwick; Brands Hatch; Case International; Caterpillar Inc.; G P Edwards; Fairoaks Airport Ltd; FLS Aerospace at London Stansted Airport; Gilmar Motor Engineers, Mark Goss; Griffiths Tucker, Liss, Hampshire; Hoverspeed, Dover; JCB; Johnston Engineering Ltd, Dorking, Surrey; Red Watch at Lambeth Fire Station, London; Lasham Gliding, Alton, Hampshire; John McCluskey; New Holland Ford Ltd; P.J.S. (Agricultural Services) Ltd, Newbury; Harbour Manager's Office at the Port of Dover; S.E.C. Fire Protection Ltd at Shepperton Studios; White Watch at Soho Fire Station, London; Blue and Green Watch at London Stansted Airport Fire Service; Ian Vickerstaff at Terex Equipment Ltd, Motherwell, Scotland. All other images © Dorling Kindersley. For further information see: **www.dkimages.com**.

The Big Book of
Things That Go

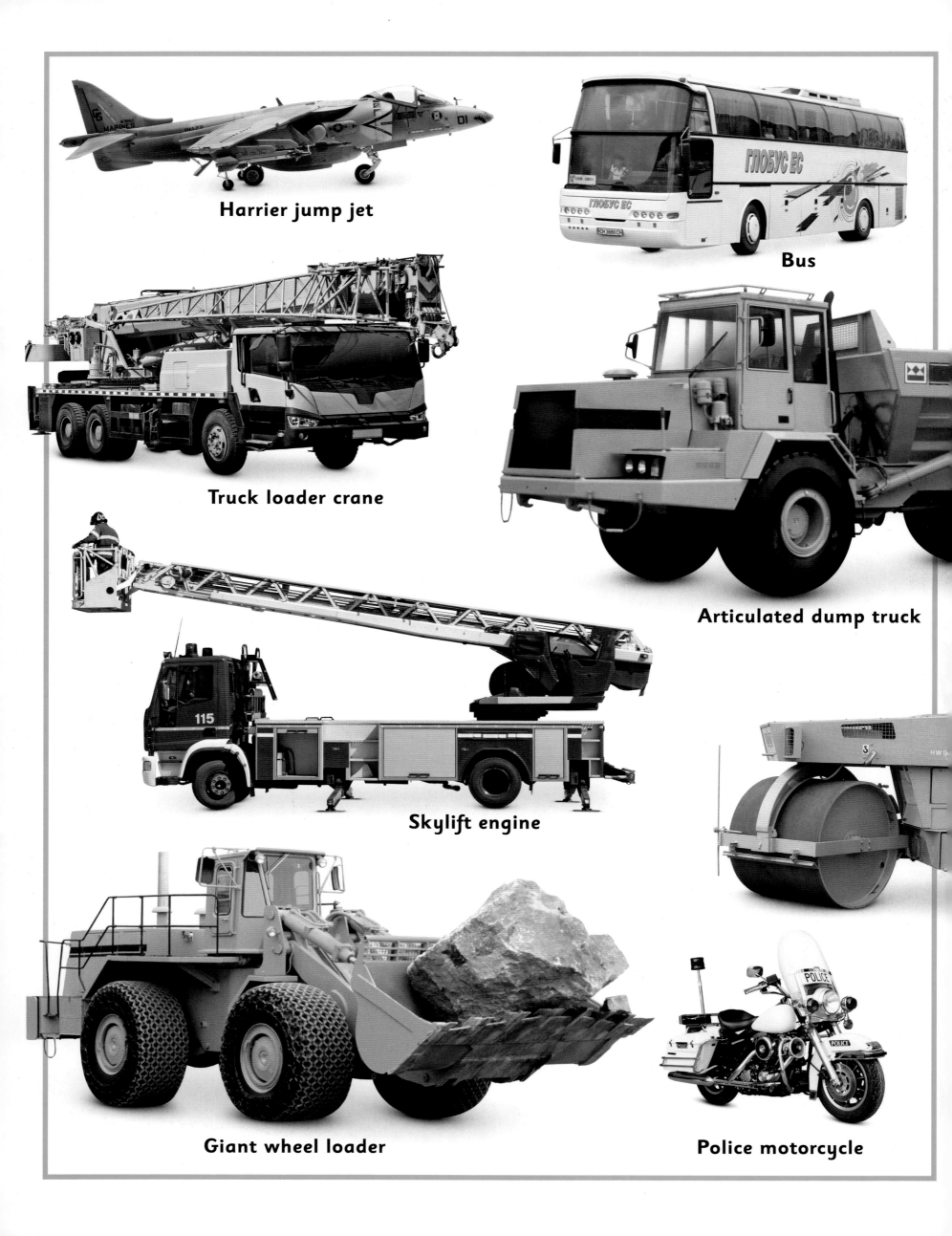

Harrier jump jet

Bus

Truck loader crane

Articulated dump truck

Skylift engine

Giant wheel loader

Police motorcycle

Contents

Hot air balloon

Multipurpose truck

Roller

Bicycle

Race car

Gondola

On the road

Car transporter

A car transporter carries many cars at one time. This one is carrying station wagons, sedans, and other types of car.

RV (recreational vehicle)

Some people go on vacation in RVs. Inside there are beds, a stove, and a bathroom.

Handlebars

Motorcycle

Motorcycles have two wheels. The rider steers with the handlebars.

Sports car

A sports car has a powerful engine. Its long, low shape helps it to zoom along at high speeds.

Bus

Buses take people on long journeys. This bus has special lockers for bags and rows of comfortable seats.

Lockers

Station wagon

A station wagon has room for a driver, four passengers, and all their bags. Luggage is stored in the large rear section.

Tanker

Tankers carry liquids in a strong metal tank. This tanker is full of milk that has been collected from a farm.

Metal tank

Pick-up truck

A pick-up truck has a flat, open back. It is useful for carrying small loads.

Trunk

Engine

Sedan

A sedan is a large, comfortable car with four doors. There is space in the trunk for luggage.

Tractor-trailer

Tractor-trailers carry all sorts of goods. The driver has a special sleeping bunk to use on long journeys.

Sleeping bunk in the back of the cab

Back door

Hatchback

This car has five doors. The fifth door is for the trunk. Hatchbacks are popular cars in cities because they are small and easy to park.

Delivery van

Delivery vans carry goods to stores and to people's homes. A sliding side door makes it easy to load up the back of the van.

Side door

City bus

People use buses to go to school or work, and to visit other places. A bus picks up its passengers at a bus stop.

Garbage truck

Garbage is often collected in trucks like this. Bags of trash are crunched up in the back of the truck.

Bicycle

Riding a bicycle is a quick way of getting around the city. Have you ever ridden a bicycle?

Saddle

Pedal

Road sweeper

A road sweeper has a big hose to suck up dirt and rubble. It is a bit like an enormous vacuum cleaner, but the road sweeper's hose is wide enough to suck up a brick!

Rubble container

Water tank

Hose

Stretch limousine

A stretch limousine is as long as two hatchbacks put together. Many limousines have a television in the back.

Light is off when taxi is occupied

YELLOW CAB
3381 305 444- 4444
Be Your Own Boss
DRIVERS WANTED
444-4444

Taxi

People take taxis to get where they need to go in a city. This is a taxi from New York City.

Rickshaw

In some countries, rickshaws are used as taxis to carry people over short distances.

Moving van

A moving van carries furniture when people move to a new home. The van is big enough to carry a whole houseful of furniture.

On rails

Steam train

Trains are pulled by engines. A steam engine driver shovels coal into a fire to heat water. The hot water turns into steam, which powers the engine and turns the wheels.

Wagon contains coal and water

Trolley car

Trolley cars are like buses that run on rails along city streets.

Diesel locomotive

This train's engine is powerful. It usually pulls up to 12 cars along the tracks.

Snowplow train

Snowplow trains use large propellers to blow away snow that has piled up on the rails.

Monorail train

Monorails run on one rail. They are used to carry people over short distances.

Sliding doors allow exit and entry at stations

Subway

Subway trains, such as this one in New York City, speed along tunnels built under the city's streets.

Rack and pinion train

The rack and pinion train can travel up and down steep hills. It has a toothy wheel that slots into a special rail, like a cog in a machine.

Driver's cab

D26

Shunter

A shunter pushes cars and goods wagons around a rail yard. It needs a powerful engine.

These buffers are used to push cars

Maglev train

The Shanghai magnetic levitation train in China travels at very high speeds without touching the rails. Magnets lift and move the train forward.

Breakdown train

The train is controlled from this cab

A breakdown train carries a giant crane. If a car comes off the rails, the crane lifts it back into position.

RS1054/50

CRANE RUNNER

At sea

Catamaran

A catamaran has two hulls. These help it to cut quickly through the waves, but make it slower to turn than single-hulled boats.

Hull

Outrigger canoe

A wooden float, or outrigger, makes this sailing boat very steady. In some countries, outrigger canoes are used for fishing.

Float

Sub-aqua craft

Sub-aqua craft are used to explore the seabed. They need powerful lamps to light the way.

Tugboat

A tugboat uses steel ropes to pull big ships into port. It can also push a ship into position using its back, or stern. This tugboat has a big tire on its stern to protect it when it bumps into other boats.

The tugboat is steered from this room, which is called the bridge

Tire

Containership

A containership carries goods in huge metal crates called containers.

Lifeboat

Funnel

Containers

MAERSK LINE

Junk

A junk is a traditional Chinese sailing ship. It has a wide, flat bottom.

Bamboo sticks, or battens, keep the sail stiff

Fishing boat

A fishing boat catches fish in a large net. The net is pulled along behind the boat.

The net is fed through this frame

P40

Two propellers drive the hovercraft forward

www.hovertravel.com

Hovercraft

A hovercraft travels over water on a cushion of air. This hovercraft can carry lots of passengers over short distances.

Ferry

People use ferries for short journeys on the ocean. This ferry has a special deck for cars and trucks.

Vehicles are parked on the lower deck

SPOKANE

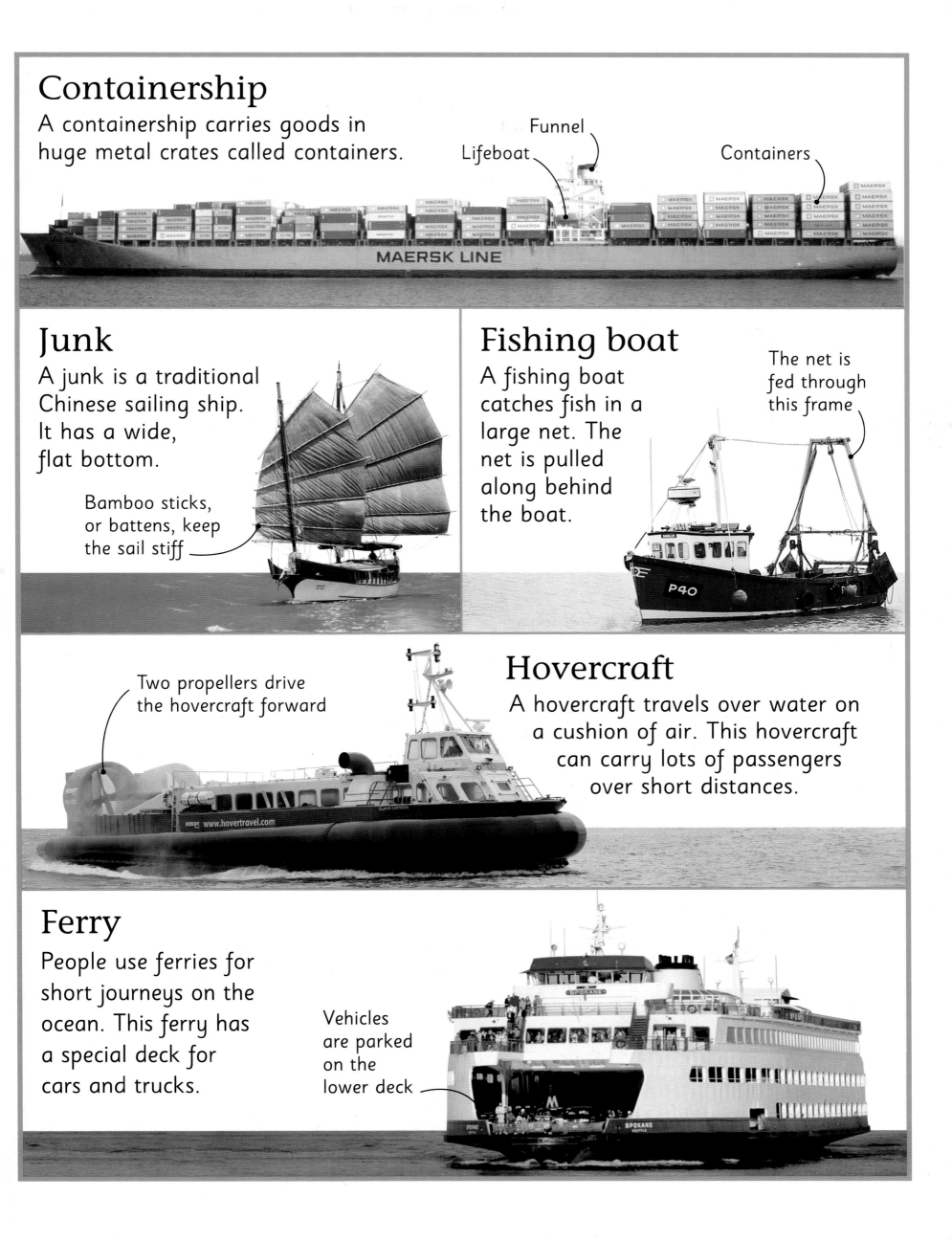

On the water

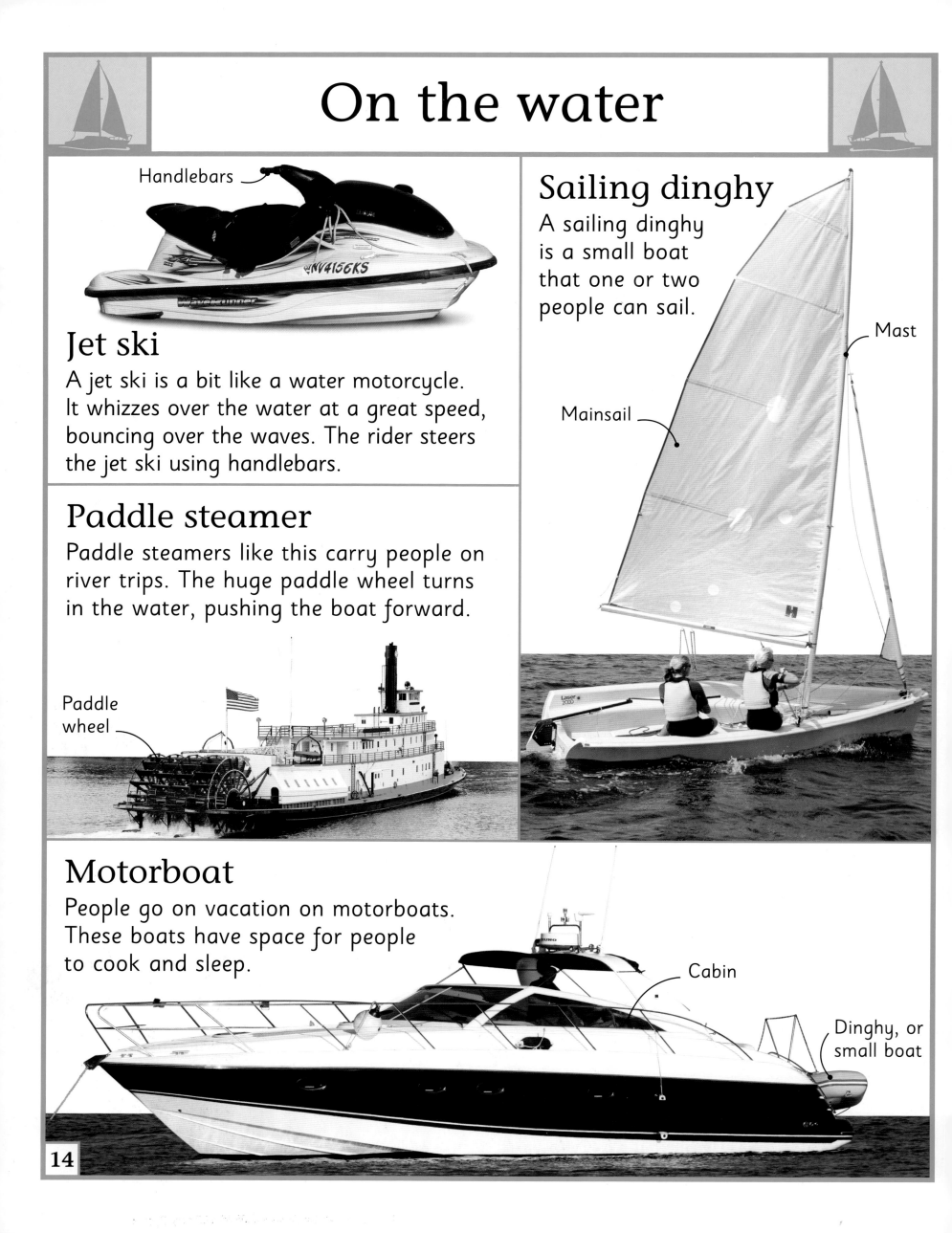

Handlebars

Jet ski

A jet ski is a bit like a water motorcycle. It whizzes over the water at a great speed, bouncing over the waves. The rider steers the jet ski using handlebars.

Paddle steamer

Paddle steamers like this carry people on river trips. The huge paddle wheel turns in the water, pushing the boat forward.

Paddle wheel

Sailing dinghy

A sailing dinghy is a small boat that one or two people can sail.

Mast

Mainsail

Motorboat

People go on vacation on motorboats. These boats have space for people to cook and sleep.

Cabin

Dinghy, or small boat

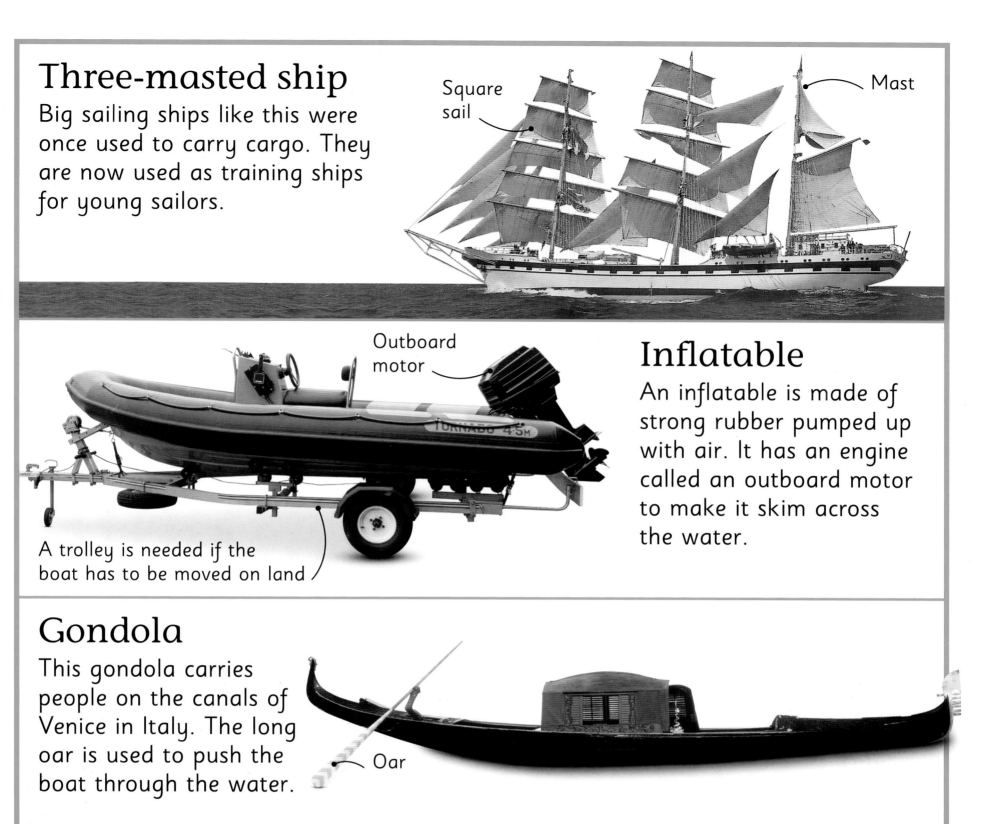

Three-masted ship

Big sailing ships like this were once used to carry cargo. They are now used as training ships for young sailors.

Square sail

Mast

Outboard motor

Inflatable

An inflatable is made of strong rubber pumped up with air. It has an engine called an outboard motor to make it skim across the water.

A trolley is needed if the boat has to be moved on land

Gondola

This gondola carries people on the canals of Venice in Italy. The long oar is used to push the boat through the water.

Oar

Ocean liner

An ocean liner is like a floating hotel. It has cabins, stores, swimming pools, and restaurants.

Swimming pool

15

In the air

Light aircraft

Light aircraft are used to carry small groups of people on short journeys.

Propeller

Cockpit

Wing

G-BEMG

Landing wheel

Rotor shaft

Rotor blade

Helicopter

A helicopter has blades instead of wings. They spin around very fast to lift the helicopter straight up into the air.

Stunt plane

A stunt plane can loop the loop and even fly upside down!

Wing

G-PITZ

Fabric wing

Propeller

Ultralight

The ultralight is a very small plane that pilots fly for fun.

Passenger plane

Passenger planes fly people all around the world, on vacations and on business. Have you ever been in a big airplane?

Tail fin

The wings of this passenger plane measure 260 ft (80 m) from tip to tip

A380

Own the sky   A380 AIRBUS

Concorde

No longer in service, this passenger jet could travel at a speed of 1,354 mph (2,179 kph), more than twice the speed of sound.

Tailfin

Movable nose section

Glider

Wing

Cockpit

The rudder is used to steer the glider

A glider has no engine. It is towed into the sky behind a light aircraft. When the tow cable is released the glider soars through the air.

Flying boat

The lower half of a flying boat is shaped like a boat's hull so that it can land on water. Small floats support its wings.

Float

Seaplane

A seaplane has floats instead of wheels so that it can take off and land on water.

Float

Burners heat the air inside the balloon

Basket

Hot air balloon

This balloon is filled with hot air, which makes it rise up into the sky. Where do you think the passengers ride?

On the farm

Tractor

A tractor is a powerful vehicle that is used to pull farm machinery. This tractor is pulling a plow to turn over the earth and bury the weeds.

Plow

Tractor with furrow press

Plowed fields are bumpy. The furrow press flattens the bumps while the power harrow smooths the earth.

Power harrow

Furrow press

Tractor with seed drill

This tractor is planting seeds. The seeds drop into the earth and are covered with soil.

Cab

Hopper contains the seeds

Cab

Tire

Multipurpose truck

This tough truck is used for different jobs on a farm. It can carry heavy loads and has deep grooves in its tires to stop it getting stuck in the mud.

Forage harvester

A forage harvester collects mown grass and chops it up. The grass is made into a cattle food called silage.

Driver's cab

Cutting blades to chop mown grass

Farm loader

This farm loader is called a Farm Master. It uses its big shovel to carry grain and cattle food around the farm.

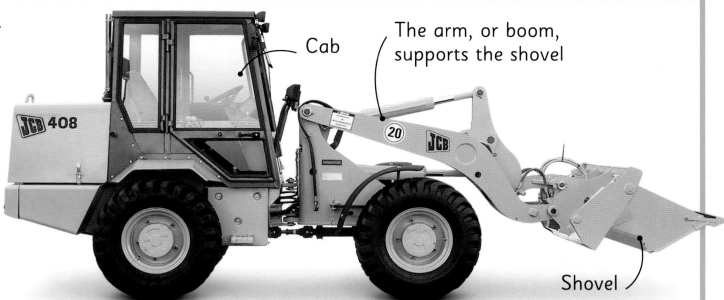

Cab

The arm, or boom, supports the shovel

Shovel

All-terrain vehicle

An all-terrain vehicle, or ATV, can travel over any sort of ground. ATVs are often used for rounding up sheep.

Combine harvester

When grain crops such as wheat, corn, and barley are fully grown they are cut, or harvested, with a combine harvester.

Grain tank

The reel pushes crops down into the cutter

Rice harvester

A rice harvester is a cutting machine. It chops down rice plants. These are collected from the field later.

Telescopic handler

Could you lift a bale of hay? It weighs about 44 lbs (20 kg). A telescopic handler can lift 64 bales of hay at a time!

The telescopic arm can extend at least 16 ft (5 m)

Hay bales are lifted on these forks

Roadwork

The legs keep the excavator steady when digging

Cab

Bucket

688B

Wheeled excavator

This excavator is like a massive shovel on wheels. Its toothy bucket digs deep trenches.

Grader

A grader has a metal blade that smooths the surface of the earth before a new road is laid.

Blade

Scraper

Blade

A scraper uses a sharp blade to cut a path through the soil. This helps to make new roads.

Compactor

A compactor has spiked wheels that squash down the earth to make it flat.

Metal plate clears a path

A canopy protects the driver from the sun and rain

Exhaust pipe

Paver

A paver spreads a layer of warm tarmac over the earth once it has been flattened.

The screed arm lays down the tarmac

The tarmac is tipped into this hopper

BG-250

Chip spreader

A chip spreader drops a thin layer of small stones over a newly laid surface of a road. The roller then presses these into the tarmac.

Mini dump truck

This truck tips out its heavy load, such as sand or gravel, wherever it is needed.

Body

Skid steer

A speedy little skid steer is useful for work where there is not much space.

Bucket

Telescopic boom

A telescopic boom has a long arm. It helps workers reach high up places, such as road lights or bridges.

Arm, or boom

Roller

A roller uses its huge wheels to flatten tarmac.

Cab

HW 90

Roller

Wheel

21

Construction site

Bulldozer

Construction sites are full of rubble. This bulldozer uses its strong steel blade to push heavy rubble aside.

Exhaust pipe

Blade

Metal crawler tracks

Rubble is carried in this skip

Dump truck

This tough little dump truck carries sand, bricks, or concrete around the site.

Articulated dump truck

An articulated dump truck carries sand, gravel, or rocks across the bumpy ground of the construction site. The dump truck body tips up to empty the load.

An articulated truck bends in the middle

Dumper body

Track excavator

This excavator has a bucket with sharp teeth. These tear into the soil to dig holes.

Arm

The tracks move easily over bumpy ground

Bucket

Bucket

Wheel loader

A wheel loader's bucket moves up and down, shoveling up earth and rocks.

Backhoe loader

A backhoe loader can dig out earth, as well as carry heavy loads.

Arm

Shovel

Bucket

Concrete mixer truck

This concrete mixer truck has a big drum that turns around and around to mix concrete. The drum is emptied through a funnel.

Fork-lift truck

A fork-lift truck is used to move heavy stacks of bricks around a site.

The prongs slide through or under objects

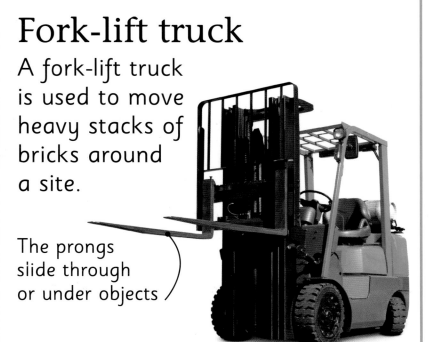

Skip loader

Skips are used as giant trash cans on sites. Special trucks collect the skips.

Crane arm

Truck loader crane

A truck loader crane has an extending crane arm. On a construction site, the crane is used to lift heavy steel bars, called girders, to each new floor of a multistorey building.

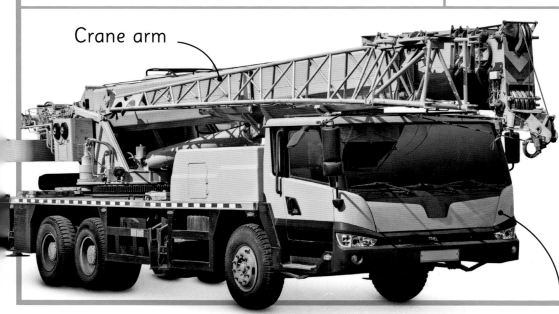

Truck cab

23

Emergency!

Police motorcycle

When police have to move fast, they can weave through traffic on a motorcycle.

Big rig tow truck

If a truck breaks down, this emergency truck might be able to help to get it moving.

This grille protects the headlights from damage

Flashing lights

Ambulance

Ambulances rush people to the hospital. This ambulance has flashing lights to tell other drivers that the ambulance is in a hurry.

Police boat

In many countries of the world, police use boats to speed across the water to help people in trouble.

MIAMI-DADE POLICE

Snowplow

A snowplow has a wide steel blade on the front to shovel snow off the road. It clears the way for cars and trucks.

Rescue helicopter

Rescue helicopters are used at sea and over mountains. A winch hoists people up into the helicopter.

Winch

Lightship

Lightships are anchored near dangerous rocks and sandbanks where a lighthouse cannot be built. The light warns other boats to keep clear.

Light

Police car

This American police car has a loud siren and flashing lights to warn other cars to let the police car pass.

Spectacles

Tow truck

This truck can tow a broken-down car to the garage. The truck lifts the car with a special frame. The frame has spectacles that slot around a car's front wheels.

Lifeboat

A lifeboat heads out to sea in stormy weather to rescue people in trouble. Radar equipment helps the crew to find a boat in distress very quickly.

Radar

Firefighters

Airport fire engine

An airport fire engine carries huge amounts of water and foam. The water and foam mixture is squirted onto a fire through the monitor.

Ladder

Monitor

This platform can hold four people

Boom

Skylift engine

A skylift engine can hoist a firefighter up to meet the flames of a fire. A water hose runs up the boom, and the firefighter points it at the flames.

Fire chief's car

This fire car races to the scene of a fire. It gets there before the other fire engines. This gives the chief fire officer time to decide how to put out the fire.

Fire rescue truck

This truck carries special firefighting equipment such as saws, hammers, and axes. It gives extra support to other fire engines.

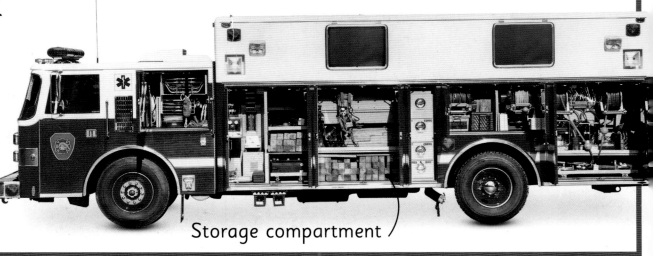

Storage compartment

Water tender engine

A water tender engine carries a tank of water. The hoses are kept rolled up, ready to be used when fighting a fire.

Hoses

Firefighting aircraft

This aircraft is fighting a forest fire. It has special water tanks that it fills by swooping down across the surface of a lake. The water tanks are emptied over the fire.

Rapid intervention vehicle

Rapid intervention vehicles like this are sometimes used at airports. They can reach a fire faster than a big truck.

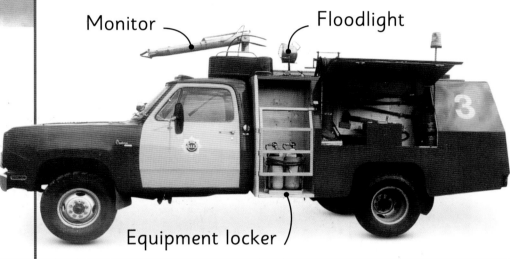

Monitor

Floodlight

Equipment locker

Articulated fire truck

The front part of this truck is joined to a trailer behind it. The whole vehicle is articulated, which means that it bends in the middle. This helps the driver steer over bumpy or muddy ground.

Trailer

Truck

At the races

Race car

A race car hugs the ground as it roars around a racetrack.

Off-road racer

Off-road racing means a bumpy ride for the driver and passenger. The cars often bounce up into the air!

Go-kart

Go-karts are small racing machines. They are driven around special tracks.

Go-kart racers must wear a helmet

Small tires

Powerboat

A powerboat has a long, narrow shape and a powerful engine. This helps it to slice through the water at top speed.

Hull

Motocross bike

Motocross bikes race over rocky and muddy ground, and up steep hills.

Racing bike

This motorcycle races at high speed on a racetrack. What differences can you see between this motorcycle and a motocross bike?

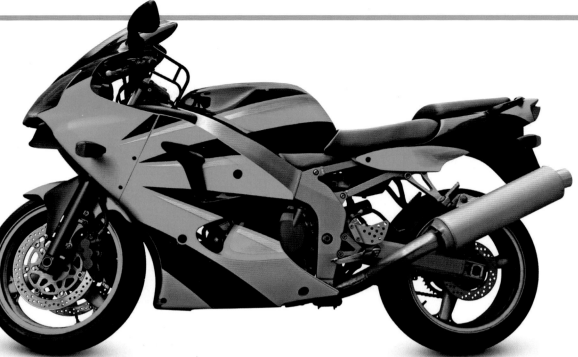

Sidecar racer

A sidecar racer takes two people. They lean from side to side to balance the bike.

Racing yacht

This racing yacht has a big crew. The crew pull on ropes called sheets to change the position of the sails. The sails catch the wind and make the yacht speed across the water.

Mast

Sail

Monster truck

These heavy vehicles can be more than 10 ft (3 m) tall. Giant wheels help them to race over rocks and crush cars.

Massive tire

Amazing machines

Giant wheel loader

This wheel loader is carrying a massive rock. The rock weighs almost as much as three large elephants!

Giant shovel

Harrier jump jet

The Harrier can rise straight up into the air. It is known as a VTOL jet, which stands for "vertical take-off and landing."

Wingtip wheel

Nose cone

Extreme motorcycle

Measuring 14 m (46 ft) in length, this is one of the longest motorcycles in the world.

This scooter can travel at a speed of 30 mph (48 kph)

Super stretch limousine

A super stretch limousine is a very long car. It has four windows running down each side.

The windows are tinted so that no one can see inside

Record-breaking car

The fastest land vehicle in the world, the jet-powered Thrust SSC, set a world land speed record of 763 mph (1,228 kph) in 1997.

One of two jet engines

Cockpit for one driver

Juggernaut

This monster juggernaut has 18 wheels. It is so heavy and makes such wide turns that it can only travel on main roads.

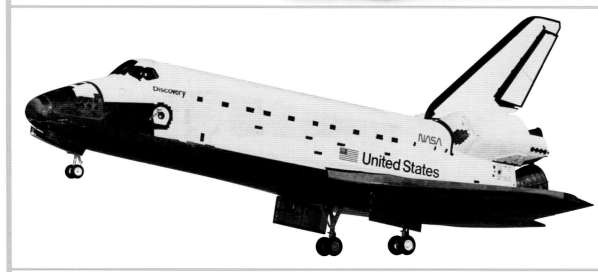

Space Shuttle

The Shuttle was the first spacecraft that could be used more than once. It had wings that helped it glide back to Earth.

Giant dump truck

If you stood next to this dump truck, you would only reach about halfway up one of the wheels. The truck is almost as tall as a house. It can carry huge loads of waste away from a construction site or quarry.

Index